THE SUN

NICK HUNTER

Heinemann
LIBRARY
Chicago, Illinois

www.capstonepub.com
Visit our website to find out more information about Heinemann-Raintree books.

To order:
☎ Phone 800-747-4992
💻 Visit www.capstonepub.com to browse our catalog and order online.

Edited by Nancy Dickmann and Laura Knowles
Designed by Steve Mead
Original illustrations © Capstone Global
    Library Ltd 2013
Picture research by Mica Brancic

Originated by Capstone Global Library Ltd
Printed and bound in China by CTPS

16 15 14 13 12
10 9 8 7 6 5 4 3 2 1

**Library of Congress Cataloging-in-
    Publication Data**
Hunter, Nick.
    The sun / Nick Hunter.—1st ed.
        p. cm.—(Astronaut travel guides)
    Includes bibliographical references and index.
    ISBN 978-1-4109-4574-7 (hb)—ISBN 978-1-
4109-4583-9 (pb) 1. Sun—Juvenile literature.
I. Title.
    QB521.5.H86 2013
    523.7—dc23   2011039070

Acknowledgements
We would like to thank the following for permission to reproduce photographs: ESA pp. 5 top and 10 (S. Corvaja, 2011), 17 (ESA/SOHO); Getty Images p. 14 (The Bridgeman Art Library/Harrogate Museums and Art Gallery, North Yorkshire, UK); Grace Wolf-Chase p. 34; Library of Congress p. 31 bottom; NASA pp. 4 (Bill Ingalls), 5 middle and 19 (SOHO (ESA & NASA)), 5 bottom and 31 top (Johnson Space Center), 7 (Phil Jones), 9 (JPL-Caltech/R. Hurt (SSC)), 20 (SOHO (ESA & NASA)), 25 (Visible Earth/EOS Project Science Office/Goddard Space Flight Center.), 26 (Goddard Space Flight Center), 37; Science Photo Library pp. 15 (Royal Astronomical Society), 18 (HR Bramaz, ISM), 23 (US Department of Energy), 28 (Detlev Van Ravenswaay), 33 (Babak Tafreshi); Shutterstock pp. 6 (© Richard Williamson), 12 (© George Bailey), 27 (James Thew), 39 (© Andriano), 40-41 (© Martiin/Fluidworkshop).

Design image elements reproduced with permission of Shutterstock/© Argus/© Igor Zh./© Reistlin Magere.

Cover photograph of a Sun plume reproduced with permission of NASA.

We would like to thank Dr. Grace Wolf-Chase, Paolo Nespoli, and the ESA for their invaluable help in the preparation of this book.

Every effort has been made to contact copyright holders of material reproduced in this book. Any omissions will be rectified in subsequent printings if notice is given to the publisher.

Disclaimer
All the Internet addresses (URLs) given in this book were valid at the time of going to press. However, due to the dynamic nature of the Internet, some addresses may have changed, or sites may have changed or ceased to exist since publication. While the author and publisher regret any inconvenience this may cause readers, no responsibility for any such changes can be accepted by either the author or the publisher.

CONTENTS

Some words are shown in bold, **like this**. You can find out what they mean by looking in the glossary.

DON'T FORGET

These boxes will remind you what you need to take with you on your big adventure.

NUMBER CRUNCHING

Don't miss these little chunks of data as you speed through the travel guide!

AMAZING FACTS

You need to know these fascinating facts to get the most out of your space safari!

WHO'S WHO?

Find out about the space explorers who have studied the universe in the past and today.

FASTEN YOUR SEAT BELT!

Today, we can travel anywhere we choose on planet Earth. However, there are only about 500 people who have ever left Earth, and only 12 people who have landed on the Moon.

What would it take to travel beyond the Moon to the planets Venus and Mars, or even to the Sun—the star at the center of our **solar system**? Spacecraft have been built that have traveled millions of miles to the edges of our solar system, but these spacecraft have not carried humans up until now.

Rockets are used to launch unmanned spacecraft into outer space. These spacecraft give us images and data about the Sun, planets, and the stars.

ROCKET POWER

The first thing you will need to travel into space is a powerful rocket. The force of **gravity** pulls us all toward Earth. To escape Earth's gravity, spacecraft need to reach speeds of 25,000 miles (40,300 kilometers) per hour. This means they need to carry a huge quantity of fuel. Being launched into space is a little like traveling in a huge bomb or firework.

STAYING ALIVE

Earth and its **atmosphere** provide everything we need to stay alive. If you are traveling in space, you will need to take all these things with you. For example, without **oxygen** to breathe, you would not survive longer than a few minutes.

Meet astronaut Paolo Nespoli on page 10.

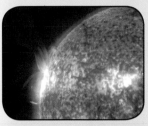

Turn to pages 20–21 to discover more about the surface of the Sun.

Find good crew members for your dangerous journey on pages 30–31.

DON'T FORGET

- Take a spacesuit with a helmet to keep you alive, especially if you are planning to leave the spacecraft.
- Exercise equipment will help you keep healthy while you are cooped up in a spacecraft.
- Bring a camera to take some great photos to show your friends when you get back!

JOURNEY TO THE SUN

People love to travel to warmer countries. But if you tried to travel to the Sun itself, you would get more than you bargained for.

HOW LONG WOULD IT TAKE?

The fastest speed ever recorded by a human-made object was the *Helios* **probe** that **orbited** the Sun in the 1970s. The probe traveled at about 150,000 miles (240,000 kilometers) per hour. At these amazing speeds, a spacecraft would take just under one month to reach the Sun, which is 93 million miles (150 million kilometers) from Earth. However, at current speeds for spacecraft carrying crew members, the journey would last around six months.

There are about 2,000 stars visible to the human eye.

ON THE WAY

There are two planets between Earth and the Sun. Both Venus and Mercury are incredibly hot. Venus's atmosphere is filled with clouds of acid that would destroy your spacecraft. Mercury has no atmosphere, meaning that it has no protection from the Sun's **energy**.

It will be even hotter closer to the Sun. In 2015, a space probe will be launched to travel closer to the Sun than ever before. It will orbit the Sun just under 4 million miles (around 6 million kilometers) above its surface. The probe will have to withstand temperatures that would melt metals such as aluminum and would be far too hot for any living things to stand.

Mercury is the closest planet to the Sun. Here you can see it passing in front of the Sun.

Mercury

THE BASICS

The Sun measures 866,000 miles (1,392,000 kilometers) in **diameter**. Earth would fit inside the Sun about one million times. The Sun sits at the center of our solar system. Eight planets travel in orbit around it—from the nearest planet, Mercury, to faraway Neptune. The Sun is also orbited by various lumps of rock or metal called asteroids or comets, some of which are big enough to qualify as **dwarf planets**.

The Sun has been shining for about 5 billion years—but don't worry, it's not going anywhere! The Sun is about halfway through its lifetime, so it should shine for another 5 billion years.

AN ATTRACTIVE DESTINATION

The planets are held in orbit around the Sun by the force of gravity. In the same way, the Moon and various human-made **satellites** go around the Earth because of gravity. Gravity holds the universe together, attracting all objects toward each other. We only really notice the force when it is exerted by massive objects like planets and stars. As you get closer to the Sun, you need to be careful and not slow down—otherwise its gravity will pull you in.

Although the Sun is huge compared to Earth and bigger than many other stars, it is not one of the biggest or brightest stars in our galaxy. The Sun is big enough to give out huge amounts of energy, which gives us the light and heat that keeps everything alive on Earth. The Sun is mostly made of **hydrogen gas**, which is the fuel that generates all its energy.

The Sun is much bigger than Earth, so its gravity is much stronger.
Here, you can see how tiny Earth is compared to the Sun.
However, they are really much farther apart.

INTERVIEW WITH AN ASTRONAUT

Paolo Nespoli is an Italian astronaut with the **European Space Agency (ESA)**. In 2007, Paolo went into space for 15 days, and in 2010 he spent 6 more months in space. In total, he has orbited Earth an amazing 2,782 times.

Q *Your very first trip into space was on a space shuttle. What did it feel like on takeoff? What were you thinking?*

A Going up in space is a risky business in a certain way, because you are strapped to a car that is going up in space propelled almost by an atomic explosion ... And on top of that you have to add the fact that you don't just go up for a fun ride—you go up to accomplish something, to accomplish some goals which are technically challenging and complex.

So what I actually felt was, on one side, some kind of happiness that the long wait and the long training was finished, this was the real thing. On the other side, I felt a little bit of apprehension. Would I perform properly as I was requested to? Would everything be okay ... or would I make a mistake about something? But everything went pretty well. You go up and nothing happens, you just enjoy the ride. It is quite an amazing feeling.

Q *When you came back from the International Space Station, was it difficult to get used to not being weightless?*

A My first ride, which was considered a short duration flight, was 15 days. Coming back, I really felt the effects of gravity pretty heavily, and so I was wondering how I would feel when I came back after six months. Now I know it's pretty bad.

I felt I weighed 200 or 300 kilograms [about 450 to 650 pounds]. Just lifting my arm was something that I needed to do consciously and pay attention to it. I mean, I had a watch on and I felt the watch was weighing 3 kilograms [about 7 pounds] on my arm! Walking was very difficult, both because of the muscles [being weak], but also because of nausea, balance problems, all sorts of things like that.

Q *If you could travel anywhere in the universe, where would you like to go, and what would you hope to find?*

A I would look for a planet somewhere that has more or less the same characteristics of Earth ... I really believe that we are not alone in the universe. I mean, if you look at the amount of stars, or planets—we are talking about millions, if not billions of planets—it's impossible, in my opinion, that there are not planets that are similar to Earth. So, I would be curious to go farther away and discovering an Earth-like planet somewhere.

DISCOVERING THE SUN

Sometime between 5,000 and 3,500 years ago, a monument made of stones, called Stonehenge, was built in southern England. No one is sure why it was built. We do know that, on the longest day of each year, the Sun rises and shines directly through the gateway of the structure.

Was Stonehenge a temple, a calendar, or a combination of the two?

ANCIENT KNOWLEDGE

Stonehenge shows that people have studied and worshipped the Sun and its movements since the earliest times. The study of stars and planets is called astronomy. Ancient people knew that the Sun gave them heat and light to live their lives and grow their crops. The path of the Sun across the sky told them the time of day and the season of the year.

Although ancient people knew the importance of the Sun, they knew little about it. They did not understand that Earth's journey around the Sun was the driving force behind our years and seasons. Nor did they know how the Sun produced so much energy. Ancient people thought the Sun orbited Earth.

WHO'S WHO?

Ptolemy (around 100–170 CE) was an astronomer who combined the knowledge of ancient Greek and Roman astronomy to predict how the stars and planets moved across the sky. His works were the basis for much of the science of astronomy for more than 1,000 years.

AMAZING FACTS

The ancient Egyptians believed the Sun was pushed across the sky by a giant scarab beetle! The idea came from scarab beetles' habit of pushing around a ball of dung containing their eggs.

COPERNICUS'S BREAKTHROUGH

It was not until 1543 that Polish astronomer Nicolaus Copernicus published his theory that Earth and all the other planets orbit the Sun. He also explained how Earth's orbit around the Sun controls the seasons.

CONTROVERSIAL THEORY

In 1609, Galileo Galilei made one of the first **telescopes**. His observations of the Sun and planets supported Copernicus's theories. This got him into trouble with the Catholic Church, which said the theory was against their teachings.

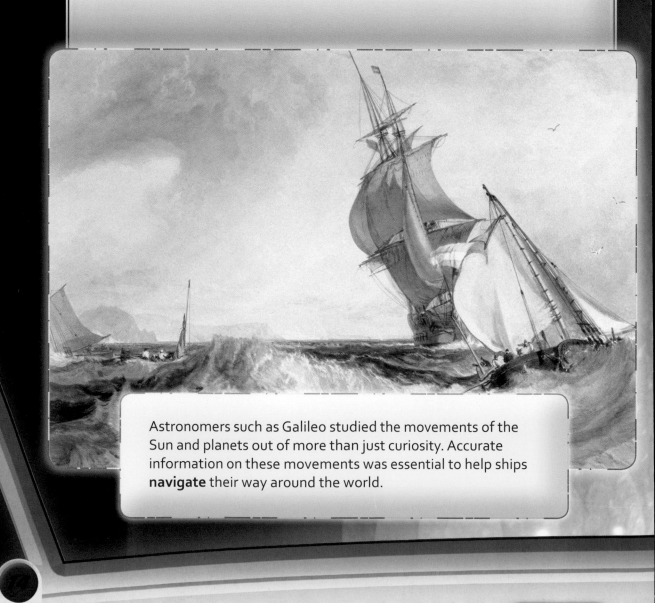

Astronomers such as Galileo studied the movements of the Sun and planets out of more than just curiosity. Accurate information on these movements was essential to help ships **navigate** their way around the world.

Galileo's work was the start of a period called the Scientific Revolution. Many discoveries were made that form the basis of modern science. Knowledge of the Sun was increasing all the time. In the late 1600s, Gian Domenico Cassini calculated the distance to the Sun, and Isaac Newton explained how the Sun's force of gravity held planets in orbit around it.

NUMBER CRUNCHING

John Herschel discovered that the Sun gives out more energy in a second than the United States uses in one year! Only a tiny fraction of this energy reaches Earth.

WHO'S WHO?

John Herschel (1792–1871) was the son of another famous astronomer, William Herschel. In addition to continuing his father's work of mapping the stars, Herschel calculated the energy produced by the Sun by measuring how it heated up water on a single square meter of Earth's surface.

STUDYING THE SURFACE

Over the centuries, astronomers were able to find out more about the features on the surface of the Sun, such as **sunspots** and **solar flares**. In the 1800s, new photographic techniques made it easier to study the Sun. Astronomers also made discoveries about what the star was made of.

Studying the Sun can be very dangerous, even from Earth! If you look directly at the Sun through a telescope without protecting your eyes, the intense glare will cause blindness. Special equipment had to be invented to study the Sun, including huge telescopes and instruments that can take detailed images of the star's surface.

DON'T FORGET

You will want to study the Sun on your trip. Here are some things that will help you:

- a dark filter that will enable you to look at the Sun without damaging your eyes
- instruments to measure the Sun's invisible but highly dangerous **radiation**
- equipment to track the waves below the surface of the Sun that tell us more about how the star works.

THE SPACE AGE

Until the 1960s, all astronomers had to view the Sun through Earth's atmosphere. Astronomers had to hope there were no clouds between them and the Sun. However, space travel meant astronomers could now use satellites and telescopes in space to learn more. Several satellites have been launched to study the Sun, including the Solar and Heliospheric **Observatory** (*SOHO*), launched in 1995, and the Solar Dynamics Observatory, launched in 2010.

However, there is still much we do not know about the Sun. If only we could get close enough to find out more!

The *SOHO* spacecraft is nearly 1 million miles (1.5 million kilometers) closer to the Sun than Earth, but it is still only one-hundredth of the distance to the Sun.

Once you have passed Mercury, things will start to get a lot hotter. The Sun is not all the same. It has several layers. The first thing you will reach is the **corona**, and it could be a bit of a shock.

CROSSING THE CORONA

The corona is the outer atmosphere of the Sun, but it is not a gentle introduction to our star. This glowing cloud of tiny gas **particles** begins as much as 1 million miles (1.6 million kilometers) from the surface of the Sun. You might think that it would be cooler, but the corona can be as hot as the center of the Sun, with temperatures reaching millions of degrees.

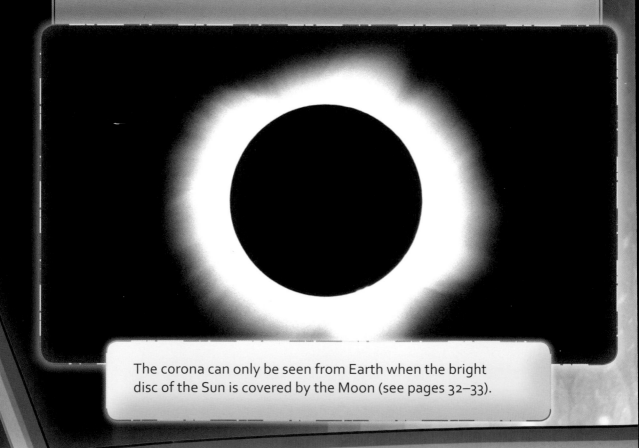

The corona can only be seen from Earth when the bright disc of the Sun is covered by the Moon (see pages 32–33).

CROSSING THE CHROMOSPHERE

If you could travel through the corona, things would cool down a little. The inner atmosphere of the Sun is called the **chromosphere**, and its temperature is about 14,000 degrees Fahrenheit (8,000 degrees Celsius). The fiery chromosphere is shaken by violent explosions called solar flares.

You may see prominences soaring up from the chromosphere. These prominences are pillars of glowing, super-heated gas. They can last for days. Eruptive prominences are violent and can soar hundreds of thousands of miles into space.

A prominence erupts from the Sun's chromosphere at a temperature of more than 108,000 °F (60,000 °C).

AMAZING FACTS

The Sun is mainly made of the gases hydrogen and **helium**. It contains 99 percent of all the **matter** in the solar system.

The Sun spins around on its **axis**, just like Earth does. Unlike Earth, different parts of the Sun rotate at different speeds, because it is not solid.

ON THE SURFACE

Beyond the chromosphere, you would reach the surface of the Sun, also known as the **photosphere**. Although it is called the surface, you could not actually land there, even if it was cool enough. The Sun's surface is made of gases rather than the rocky crust of planets like Earth. The photosphere is where the heat and light that radiate out into the solar system come from, and it is the part of the Sun that can be seen from Earth.

New material is constantly rising to the surface from the Sun's core.

WHAT DOES THE SURFACE LOOK LIKE?

When you get closer to the surface, it appears to be covered in patches of different colors. These patches are caused by the streams of incredibly hot material rising up from the Sun's **core** to the relatively cool surface. Of course, at around 9,900 degrees Fahrenheit (5,500 degrees Celsius), it is not that cool. The photosphere will also feature darker patches called sunspots.

The Sun is much bigger than other objects in the solar system. Bigger or more massive objects have stronger forces of gravity. The gravity on the Sun's surface is 28 times that felt on Earth, so you would weigh 28 times as much. Humans can withstand this level of gravity, or g force, for a few seconds, but any longer would result in death.

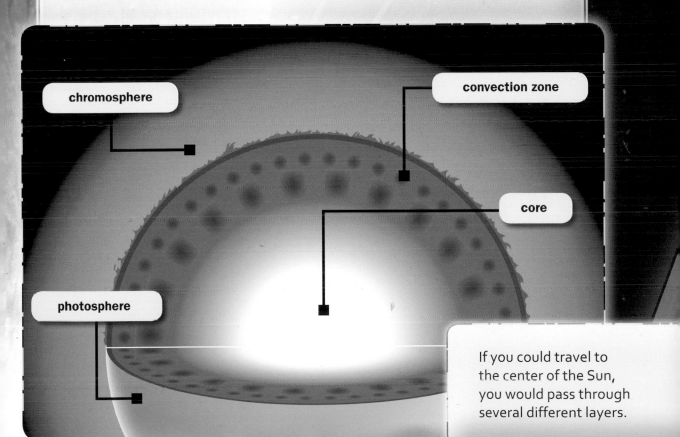

chromosphere

convection zone

core

photosphere

If you could travel to the center of the Sun, you would pass through several different layers.

TO THE CORE

The core of the Sun is where the action happens. At temperatures of around 27 million degrees Fahrenheit (15 million degrees Celsius), the Sun generates the energy that provides light and heat to Earth and all the other planets in the solar system. The light and heat take hundreds of thousands of years to make their way from the core to the surface.

The Sun generates this energy by a process called **nuclear fusion**. **Atoms** are the tiny units that make up all matter. At incredibly high temperatures, the hydrogen atoms that make up most of the Sun can fuse (join) together to make helium. When this happens, energy is released. When millions of tons of hydrogen atoms are fusing in the Sun every second, the amount of energy released is enormous.

AMAZING FACTS

Controlled nuclear fusion could be a way to generate power on Earth. It releases huge amounts of energy, but it does not produce harmful waste like existing nuclear energy. The problem is that the fusion process needs very high temperatures, like those found at the core of the Sun.

The massive blast of a hydrogen bomb is created by an uncontrolled fusion reaction—a very small version of what happens inside the Sun.

UNDER PRESSURE

The atoms are under huge pressure because of the size of the Sun. They are pressed together until they have a **density** 150 times greater than water. This means that if we could collect a teaspoon of matter from the Sun, it would have 150 times the **mass** of a teaspoon of water. Even if it were possible to find a material that could stand the heat of the core, it would be crushed by this enormous pressure.

WHEN TO GO

There is an old joke that the best time to go to the Sun is at night. Of course, the Sun is always shining, even when we cannot see it. There is not really a good time to go. The Sun is always incredibly hot, but the temperature on the surface is not always the same.

SUNSPOTS

Since people first studied the Sun, they have noticed dark patches called sunspots appearing on the surface. These spots are cooler areas on the Sun's surface that are caused by disturbances inside the Sun. The good news for travelers is that they are cooler than the rest of the photosphere. The bad news is that they are still hot enough to melt any spacecraft.

AMAZING FACTS

In previous centuries, astronomers thought that sunspots were so cool that people may be able to land on them. William Herschel (1738–1822) suggested that they were openings in the Sun's atmosphere.

Sunspots are made up of a dark central area called the umbra, surrounded by a lighter area called the penumbra.

SEASONS ON THE SUN

While sunspots may look small compared to the huge size of the Sun, many are bigger than Earth. They change size as they move across the photosphere. Samuel Heinrich Schwabe (1789–1875) was an amateur German astronomer. He observed that the number and size of sunspots followed a pattern that repeated itself about every 11 years. These patterns give the Sun "seasons." Although sunspots themselves are cooler, more heat reaches Earth from the Sun when there is greater sunspot activity.

SOLAR FLARES

Solar flares are huge eruptions of gas from the Sun. Flares are most common at times of the greatest sunspot activity and can reach temperatures of up to 180 million degrees Fahrenheit (100 million degrees Celsius). If you want to avoid encountering a solar flare, you should travel when there are fewer sunspots.

WIND FROM THE SUN

Solar flares do not just affect the area around the Sun. Their impact is felt on Earth and across the solar system. The solar wind is a constant flow of radiation and atomic particles from the Sun out into the solar system. Solar flares throw out massive quantities of these particles, making the solar wind even stronger.

Astronomers are able to see amazing pictures of solar flares because of special space telescopes on satellites.

Earth's magnetic field and atmosphere protect us from the solar wind. However, the solar wind's effects can be seen in the Northern and Southern Lights (*Aurora borealis* and *Aurora australis*). These shimmering patterns of light appear close to the North and South Poles, at the northern and southern ends of Earth's axis.

DON'T FORGET

You will need to make sure your spacecraft has the right protection for your long journey in space, since you will not have Earth's atmosphere to shield you from the solar wind. Scientists are developing a magnetic shield that will protect spacecraft and astronauts from radiation in the solar wind.

The Northern and Southern Lights are the only signs of the solar wind that we can see from Earth.

WHO'S WHO?

Richard Carrington (1826–1875) made a major contribution to our understanding of the Sun from his private observatory. He noted the connection between a huge solar flare and changes in the solar wind.

LOOKING TO THE FUTURE

Maybe the best thing to do would be to wait until the Sun cools down before traveling there. As the hydrogen atoms join together to power the Sun, some of their mass is changed into energy. The Sun loses about 4 million tons of its mass every second in the form of energy.

The Sun probably has enough fuel to last another 5 billion years. When its fuel starts to run out, the Sun will collapse in on itself, because of the force of its gravity. This will cause it to become even hotter than before, as the fusion reactions continue. Then, the reheated star will expand to become a red giant many times bigger than now.

Even Earth may be swallowed up by the expanding Sun in its red giant phase.

WHITE DWARF

After millions of years, only a small white core, called a white dwarf, will be left behind. Over billions of years, the white dwarf will cool down. That might be a good time to visit. But, even if Earth has not been swallowed or burned to a crisp by the dying Sun, humans would not be able to survive without its heat and light.

White dwarf stars fit a huge amount of mass into a very small space. This makes them have an extremely high density. If you could fill a 1-liter bottle with material from a white dwarf, it would weigh about 1,000 tons!

1. Like other stars, the Sun began life inside a swirling cloud of gas and dust called a nebula. A clump of gas and dust formed and grew larger and larger. Gravity pulled the material closer together.

2. The pressure and temperature at the center of the clump grew. When it got hot enough, nuclear fusion reactions started. Energy was released into space, and the Sun started to shine.

3. The new Sun burned brightly for millions of years. This is the stage our Sun is at now. As it gets older, its fuel will begin to run out and it will become less bright. A medium-sized star like our Sun shines for around 10 billion years. More massive stars use up their fuel more quickly, so they have shorter lives.

6. The white dwarf cools down and stops shining. It becomes a black dwarf and is almost invisible.

5. The material left behind will shrink to form a white dwarf. White dwarfs are about the size of a planet, but they are very dense.

4. As the Sun's fuel runs out, the dying Sun will get bigger and become a red giant. Its outer layers of gas will start to escape into space.

Astronomers know about the likely future of the Sun from studying the fate of similar stars.

WHO'S GOING WITH YOU?

You will be lucky to find anyone to go with you on this mission to the Sun. Don't take any of your friends— a mission that involves certain doom will not make you popular with them. No one has ever been to the Sun, so you won't be able to take a good guide.

CREW MEMBER:

GALILEO GALILEI (1564–1642)

Galileo would be the first to volunteer for any mission to the Sun. He was not afraid to take risks when he proved the theory that the Earth goes around the Sun, going against the wishes of the Catholic Church at the time. If he were alive today, he would probably be looking for new ways to find out about the Sun.

POTENTIAL JOB:

Engineer

CREW MEMBER:

NUCLEAR PHYSICIST

Take someone who understands how nuclear fusion works—a nuclear physicist. Your journey could have real value if you can learn enough to help develop controlled nuclear fusion on Earth.

POTENTIAL JOB:

Scientific observer

CREW MEMBER:

ASTRONAUT

Great scientists are very important, but on a journey like this you will need an experienced astronaut who knows what he or she is doing. It is a long way to the Sun, so you want a companion who has spent a long time in space, maybe working on the International Space Station.

POTENTIAL JOB:

Pilot

CREW MEMBER:

ALBERT EINSTEIN (1879–1955)

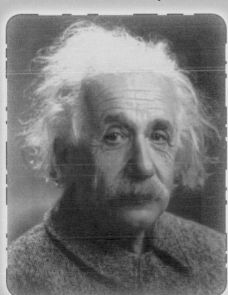

Einstein probably did more to explain how physics works in space than anyone else. He developed theories about the behavior of light and the impact of gravity on large bodies, such as stars. Although many of Einstein's ideas were based on theory, they have since been proved by experiments.

POTENTIAL JOB:

Navigator

Even if it is impossible to visit the Sun, there is plenty you can find out without leaving Earth. One spectacle involving the Sun is rare but amazing.

TOTAL ECLIPSE

While Earth is orbiting the Sun, the Moon orbits Earth. A solar eclipse happens when the Moon comes between Earth and the Sun in its orbit. The face of the Sun is partly or completely covered by the Moon. For the few seconds to a few minutes when the Sun's face is totally covered, the sky turns dark. This is a total eclipse. Then, the Sun starts to become visible again.

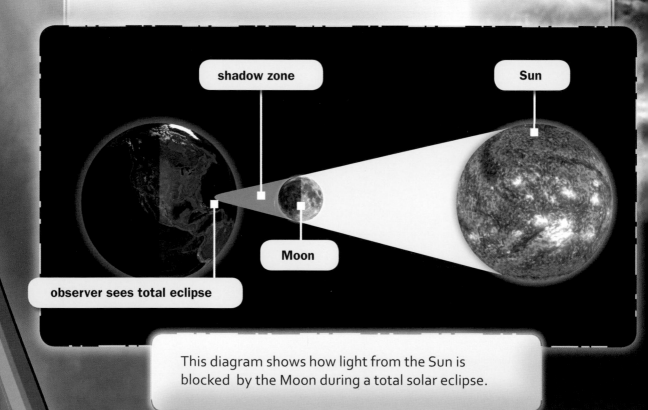

shadow zone

Sun

Moon

observer sees total eclipse

This diagram shows how light from the Sun is blocked by the Moon during a total solar eclipse.

Total solar eclipses happen because the face of the Sun is 400 times larger than the Moon, but it is also 400 times farther away, so the two look the same size.

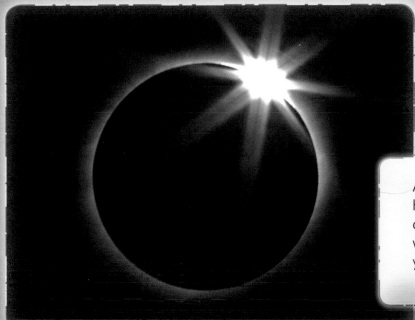

A total eclipse only happens once every one or two years. You will be very lucky if you see one!

You should never look directly at the Sun during an eclipse, particularly through a device such as telescope or camera. But don't be scared away! To view the eclipse safely, make sure you have:

- a filter that is approved for viewing the Sun
- a way of projecting the eclipse onto a screen for viewing— for example, by using a pinhole projector.

INTERVIEW WITH AN ASTRONOMER

Dr. Grace Wolf-Chase is an astronomer at the Adler Planetarium in Chicago, Illinois. She tries to discover how cold clouds of gas and dust collapse in space to form the different kinds of stars that we see in the sky.

Q *Why are you interested in the formation of stars?*

A I'm interested in how stars form because this tells us a lot about how our star, the Sun, and its planets (including Earth) formed. Understanding how different types of stars and planets form might tell us a lot about the conditions that lead to the development of life.

Q *What is the most interesting thing you have learned about stars?*

A It's that many of them have planets that orbit them just as the Earth orbits the Sun. When I was in school, we only knew about the planets in our solar system. Since 1995, we have discovered over 680 planets orbiting other stars, and this number just keeps increasing. In fact, it's possible that most stars have planets. This means there may be a huge number of planets that are similar to Earth in the universe!

Q *Do you think that there is life elsewhere in the universe?*

A I think it's extremely likely, for two main reasons. Firstly, we've discovered that many stars have planets, and it seems likely that at least some of these planets have the right conditions for life to exist. Secondly, we've discovered that life on Earth is incredibly diverse. Many organisms can survive in environments that humans consider "extreme," such as very high or low temperatures or pressures. So it seems reasonable that there might be many environments in the universe that are capable of supporting life.

Q *Which historical astronomer would you most like to meet and talk to?*

A There are many astronomers that haven't made it into the history books. I wish the names and lives of more women astronomers had been preserved through time! Because of this, I'd probably want to meet Caroline Herschel, since she is one of the few historical women astronomers whose life is well documented. She was born in 1750 and lived to the age of 98! She lived and worked with her brother, William, who was also an astronomer. Caroline discovered several comets and nebulae. She helped her brother to build telescopes and to develop a mathematical approach to astronomy.

LIVING ON THE SUN?

The first and most obvious reason why we could not live on the Sun is the incredible heat. The highest temperature ever measured on Earth is 136 degrees Fahrenheit (58 degrees Celsius), whereas the temperature on the Sun varies from a few thousand to millions of degrees. Even in the coolest parts of the Sun's atmosphere, solid materials like metals would be turned to gas.

Even if we ignore the intense heat, the Sun is made up almost entirely of hydrogen and helium. One of the main reasons why we can live on Earth is because the atmosphere contains oxygen for living things to breathe. Oxygen combines with hydrogen to make water, which is also essential for living things.

DON'T FORGET

Human beings and other animals need the following things to survive:

- oxygen to breathe
- water, which makes up about 60 percent of the human body and is needed to regulate body temperature and make the body function
- food to give us energy.

These things are not found on the Sun, so you will need to take them with you when traveling in space.

Astronauts on the International Space Station have proved that people can stay in space for long periods, but they are only 240 miles (386 kilometers) from Earth.

RADIATION RISK

The Sun does not just produce heat and light. The solar wind also carries radiation and charged particles across the solar system. Earth's atmosphere protects us from this harmful radiation. The radiation can damage living cells, even at a distance of 93 million miles (150 million kilometers) from the Sun.

LIVING WITHOUT THE SUN

Although we could not live on the Sun, we certainly could not live without it. The Sun is the source of nearly all the energy on Earth.

NEITHER TOO NEAR, NOR TOO FAR

Earth is the right distance from the Sun, so that water normally exists as a liquid on the surface. Earth is the only planet where this is the case. If we were any farther from the Sun, our climate would be much colder, water would freeze, and we would not have the water we need to survive.

The Sun's warmth and light helps plants to grow, and these feed humans and other animals. To understand how delicate this balance is, we only have to look at Earth's extremes. Very few things grow near the North and South Poles, because the climate is too cold and dry. In deserts, the climate is too hot and dry for many things to grow.

NUMBER CRUNCHING

Other planets experience very extreme temperatures because they are nearer or farther from the Sun. The average temperature on Mercury is 831 degrees Fahrenheit (444 degrees Celsius). On distant Neptune, it is a chilly –330 degrees Fahrenheit (–201 degrees Celsius).

The energy that these potato plants absorb from the Sun transfers to us when we eat them.

CHANGING CLIMATE

Scientists have shown that the actions of humans are changing this balance. Fumes from cars and industry are changing our atmosphere so that it is allowing less of the Sun's heat to escape. Our climate is becoming warmer, and many people believe that this could upset the balance of Earth's relationship with the Sun.

MAP OF THE SOLAR SYSTEM

MERCURY

VENUS

EARTH

MARS

ASTEROID BELT

JUPITER

SATURN

URANUS

NEPTUNE

The sizes of the planets and their distances from the Sun are not to scale. To show all the planets' real distances from the Sun, this page would have to be over half a mile long!

TIMELINE

Around 5 billion years ago
The Sun and planets of the solar system form.

3000–1520 BCE
Stonehenge is built in southern England in several stages.

1543 CE
Nicolaus Copernicus publishes the theory that Earth orbits around the Sun.

1609
Galileo makes his first observations with a telescope.

1670s
Cassini calculates the distance to the Sun.

1687
Isaac Newton publishes his theories of how gravity holds the planets in orbit around the Sun.

1838
John Herschel conducts experiment to measure the Sun's energy.

1843
Samuel Heinrich Schwabe discovers that sunspots follow a pattern, or cycle, every 11 years.

1859
Richard Carrington observes a solar flare for the first time.

1959
The *Luna 1* spacecraft detects the solar wind.

1961
Astronaut Yuri Gagarin pilots the first manned spaceflight.

1962–1975
NASA launches a series of Orbiting Solar Observatories to study the Sun.

1995
The *SOHO* probe is launched into orbit around the Sun.

2010
The Solar Dynamics Observatory (SDO) is launched. It observes the Sun every 10 to 50 seconds, to see small changes that previous probes could not capture.

FACT FILE

POSITION:
Outer region of the Milky Way galaxy

DISTANCE FROM EARTH:
93 million miles (150 million kilometers). Light from the Sun takes about 8 minutes to reach Earth

SIZE:
866,000 miles (1,392,000 kilometers) in diameter

MASS:
330,000 times greater than the mass of Earth

TEMPERATURE:
- Surface: 9,900 degrees Fahrenheit
            (5,500 degrees Celsius)
- Core: 27 million degrees Fahrenheit
            (15 million degrees Celsius)

MADE FROM:
- Hydrogen: 71 percent
- Helium: 27 percent
- Other gases: 2 percent

SATELLITES:
Eight planets orbit around the Sun (Mercury, Venus, Earth, Mars, Jupiter, Saturn, Uranus, Neptune), plus at least three dwarf planets and many other asteroids and comets

GLOSSARY

atmosphere layer of gases surrounding a planet

atom smallest unit of matter that makes up everything

axis imaginary line around which something rotates, such as a planet

chromosphere inner part of the Sun's atmosphere, above the visible surface

core center of the Sun

corona outer part of the Sun's atmosphere

density amount of matter, or mass, contained in a volume

diameter width of a circle at its widest point

dwarf planet object that orbits the Sun but is smaller than the eight recognized planets, such as Pluto

energy capacity to do work

European Space Agency (ESA) European organization involved in space research and exploration

gas matter, such as oxygen, that is able to expand without limit unless it is contained

gravity force that pulls objects toward each other. Big objects, such as planets, have much stronger gravity than smaller objects, such as people.

helium gas lighter than air, formed when two hydrogen atoms fuse in the core of the Sun

hydrogen lightest and most abundant element in the solar system, which makes up most of the Sun

mass amount of material that makes up an object

matter anything that has mass and fills space, including solids, liquids, and gases

NASA short for "National Aeronautics and Space Administration," the U.S. space agency

navigate find the way, particularly when at sea or in the air

nuclear fusion process in which hydrogen atoms join together to make new atoms

observatory building with telescopes and other instruments for observing (looking at) stars and planets

orbit path of an object around a star or planet

oxygen gas present in Earth's atmosphere that most living things need to breathe

particle tiny part, such as part of an atom

photosphere surface of the Sun, normally visible from Earth

probe unmanned spacecraft designed to send back data and images of space

radiation tiny particles, smaller than an atom, emitted (thrown out) by the Sun

satellite object, often human-made, that orbits a larger object

solar flare sudden and violent release of matter and energy from the Sun

solar system the Sun, the planets, and other objects that are in orbit around the Sun

sunspot darker area on the surface of the Sun

telescope instrument that makes distant objects look bigger

FIND OUT MORE

BOOKS

Bond, Peter. *DK Guide to Space* (DK Guides). New York: Dorling Kindersley, 2006.

Goldsmith, Mike. *Solar System* (Discover Science). New York: Macmillan, 2010.

Mist, Rosalind. *Will the Sun Ever Burn Out? Earth, Sun, and Moon* (Stargazers' Guides). Chicago: Heinemann Library, 2006.

Parker, Steve. *The Sun* (Earth and Space). New York: Rosen Central, 2008.

INTERNET SITES

FactHound offers a safe, fun way to find internet sites related to this book. All of the sites on FactHound have been researched by our staff.

Here's all you do:

Visit *www.facthound.com*

Type in this code: 9781410945747

PLACES TO VISIT

Hayden Planetarium
Central Park West and 79th Street, New York, N.Y. 10024
www.haydenplanetarium.org

Smithsonian National Air and Space Museum
Independence Ave. at 7th St. SW, Washington, D.C. 20560
www.nasm.si.edu

SIGHTS TO SEE

If you get the chance, you should try to see a solar eclipse. These happen rarely and can only be seen from certain places. Other Sun-related sights you might be able to see include the *Aurorae*, which appear in the extreme north and south of our planet.

FURTHER RESEARCH

- Stars: The Sun is just one of billions of stars in the universe. There is plenty you can find out about other stars and amazing things like supernovas and black holes.
- Scientists: People like Galileo and Newton made amazing discoveries that helped us understand more about the Sun. You can find out more about their lives and discoveries and the many other advances of the Scientific Revolution.
- Effects of the Sun on Earth: Research the different ways that Earth's relationship with the Sun affects people and living things, from seasons and energy to how we measure time.

WARNING

Make sure that you never look directly at the Sun. Although you can look at stars through binoculars or a telescope, you must never use these to look at the Sun. Looking at the Sun can damage your eyes.

INDEX